THEY CALL ME STARLIGHT

THEY CALL ME STARLIGHT

A TRUE STORY OF HORSE AND HUMAN, HEARTACHE AND HEALING

DAWN M. SMITH

To

Tiffany Smith, horse whisperer, dreamer,
healer, and eternal optimist

and to Elliott Smith, "horse-girl husband",
who lovingly supports her passion for all
animals (especially horses)

Love you both

TABLE OF CONTENTS

Introduction...1

My Story Begins 3

Secretariat Center 8

I Make a Choice 13

Home in Indiana 19

Lola 25

Dream Horse 28

Sage 32

Bandit..36

Dance Lessons...39

Friends 43

Finding Myself...48

Learning to be Brave 52

Setback...59

Thanksgiving and New Year.......................................64

Beacon Hill 69

Secrets...76

Nugget 79

Dragon Queen...82

Redemption...86

Miracles...92

From the Author..96

References and End Notes.. 100

Acknowledgements.. 102

Introduction

Horses do not judge humans, they judge our behavior, including our most subtle intentions. A horse will consistently mirror back the exact feelings, attitudes, and intentions of a human that initiates even the slightest interaction. -Tim Hayes, Huffpost, The Blog 12-3-16

Horses change lives. They give our young people confidence and self-esteem. They provide peace to troubled souls – they give us hope. -Toni Robinson

The natural ability of horses to read and reflect human emotions has been studied and well-established, and is the basis for many versions of equine-based therapy, both physical and emotional. In working with horses, people find they can work through challenges and improve their physical and emotional health. The intuitive nature of the horse, a herd animal, fosters cooperation and sociability, and reaches inside a person at an unspoken level, to uncover deeply hidden issues and work through them.

But, what if the horse itself has developed deep issues — has in essence forgotten how to be a horse? Is it possible for human-horse interaction to help the horse, the way horses so often help people? Here is a horse with a story to tell, and just maybe the telling will resonate with someone who feels the same struggles she faces.

The animals, people, places and events in this story are all real, although some names have been changed to protect privacy. The only conjecture is the inner thought of the horse, as we all know that horses can't really talk — except perhaps to those who listen with the heart.

-1-

My Story Begins

A horse is worth more than riches   *-Spanish proverb*

They call me Starlight. Such a lovely name, invoking brightness and beauty. I am a horse, a thoroughbred mare, such a dark brown that my glossy coat looks black in most light. I have a crooked star on my forehead, and a thin white stripe down my nose. My mane, tail, and legs are black, except for a white fetlock on my left rear leg. I am tall and thin, classic thoroughbred conformation, and yes, I know that I am physically beautiful. But, external beauty does not always match what is inside.

I was a racehorse. My training began when I was very young, just a yearling. I must admit, it was initially exciting, exhilarating. I was the center of attention. There were crowds and noise and the thrill of running, and sometimes the joy of winning. I could feel the pride and excitement of the humans when I won. I would prance and circle and show off, and glory in the praise of the people around me. I wanted to do it more, please them more. It became an addiction. But in time, the true darkness of the addiction emerged.

I loved to run, but I never showed the talent to be trained for the big stakes races, or even the allowance races*. I was placed in several allowance races early in my career, but did not do well, so I was returned to claiming* races. Since the nature of claiming races allows the horse to be claimed by a different owner at the end of the race, I often found my world to change after a race.

During my 4-1/2 years racing, I ran 52 races, earning a total of $107,836.00. I won 7 races, placed second 12 times and third 7 times. I had four owners, 17 jockeys, and went to 11 racetracks. This resulted in some very confusing outcomes for me. There were times that I did not run well, felt sad because I could feel the disappointment of the humans around me, so I wanted to do better. When I ran very well, I achieved the high of winning and being praised and hearing the cheers of the humans, but if I happened to have been claimed in that race, everything would suddenly change. My previous owner received my winnings, and I went to a new home. All this became very unsettling. I craved the high of the win, a type of addiction, but feared the possibility of going

*See References and End Notes

to a new home, or of having a new jockey just when I was doing well, or going into a different training program, all of which confused me. Sometimes I would win and was not claimed, so would return to the same home, and I would be very happy. But, just about the time I began to believe that I finally achieved stability, it would all change again.

Over time, the exhilaration of running morphed to anxiety. I did not always win, and when I did not finish at least in the top three, the disappointment of my humans knifed through me, as I knew I had let them down. I wanted to feel the high of the win, but I could not always achieve it. Early in my career there had been excitement and anticipation of the start of the race and the hope for the high of the win at the finish. Slowly, it became fear, anxiety, and reluctance that I might possibly feel the frustration of loss or the disruption of being claimed. Where once, I would prance to the gate, I started dancing in fear. But my handlers did not feel the difference, or did not care, and kept taking me to the gate.

There was a specific physical alteration as well. I was a "roarer". My breathing as I ran was noisy, due to a condition that is somewhat common in tall, long-necked horses like thoroughbreds. The condition involves lack of function of the nerve that controls one of the flaps of tissue that opens and closes the airway, preventing the airway from opening all the way during exercise. This partially blocks the airway, resulting in the typical roaring noise. It also reduces airflow, so tolerance for exercise is reduced, and in racehorses like me, it can significantly reduce racing ability. The good news is there is a simple surgery to help open the airway better. It involves a stitch that holds the floppy tissue permanently open[3]. The bad news is that this results in the inability to make a loud noise. I could no longer whinny out loud; all I can muster is a soft nicker. For a herd animal, losing voice is devastating. I can no longer call to or answer my friends. I can no longer sing.

Racehorses cannot race forever, and my racing career ended after four and a half years. I had such warring emotions about it all. I was relieved because I no longer had to face the anxiety of the races, but at the same time, there would never again be the high of the win. I had no way to achieve the high I craved. But, neither did I have to face the disappointment, and these conflicting emotions caused me great stress. I sometimes felt the conflict inside would burst into flame that all could see, but that flame turned inward. By the time of my racing retirement, I had stomach ulcers. The humans wanted to breed me, and tried hormone treatments, but that just made my physical condition worse, and I never was successfully bred.

By the time I left the track, I was a physical and emotional wreck – anxious, depressed, ulcers, hormone imbalance, infertile. I was worth something to humans when I might win them money or give them a foal. Ultimately, I became useless.

They call me Starlight, but all I feel is darkness.

-2-

Secretariat Center

It is the difficult horses that have the most to give you.
-Lendon Gray

May 18, 2016. It has been a little over five months since my last race. Breeding was not successful. I have been brought to a place called Secretariat Center. This is a facility at the Kentucky Horse Park in Lexington, Kentucky, that works with retired thoroughbreds to retrain and rehome us. The goal is to find the right match between the horse and the new owner, to assure that the horse can live a happy, healthy life after racing. Most retired thoroughbreds go on to become mounts for pleasure riding, or jumping, or dressage, or show horses. Secretariat Center is bright and cheerful and set amid large paddocks of lush bluegrass. There are rolling hills and a warm, sweet breeze. The barn has spacious, clean stalls.

The humans here are caring and considerate. And, in my depression, I am oblivious.

The human who directs my training is Susannah. She speaks softly and calmly, but I do not understand what is required of me. Surely something is required of me, as I've been trying to meet someone's expectations all my life. By now, my anxiety manifests in multiple nervous mannerisms. If I am in the crossties more than just a few minutes, I start pawing the ground. I know it is not desirable behavior, but I cannot help myself. I don't know what is going to happen and I have to move to keep myself from exploding. I don't really like to be groomed, and especially dislike having my chest, belly, ears, or face touched. I grind my teeth and pin my ears and try to bite, not because I want to be mean or bad, but just because I am anxious and scared and just want to be left alone. I know it is irrational, but that is what anxiety is – nebulous, irrational fear that slips through any effort to contain it. I hate feeling this way, and I know it worries Susannah, because I hear her tell the others that it seems like I have forgotten how to be a horse.

At first, that seems to me to be a silly thing to say. Of course I am a horse, look at me! And then I realize I am standing alone in a corner of the paddock, even though there are other horses out here. I realize this actually is odd behavior. Horses are herd animals; we like to be chummy. But that thought comes to me in such a detached way, as I stand alone, head down, not really even very interested in eating. That is also very un-horse-like; we normally graze all day. Detached is right. I am detached, alone, no purpose, just tired. Sad. Maybe I *have* forgotten how to be a horse. But it doesn't really matter, does it? Just leave me alone.

After some time at Secretariat Center, with the devoted care of Susannah and her staff, my ulcers are healing, my appetite is improving, and I am a little calmer than I was when I first arrived. I have been treated to massages, acupuncture, and other "spa" treatments. I pal around with some of the other horses now, although I still tend to be a loner. Susannah says I am an "angry mare", although there is no condemnation in her voice as she says it, just sadness and concern. She and the others have been working with me with groundwork and riding, trying to develop me into a reliable mount.

I really do want to please them, but sometimes things erupt and I lose control. I have bolted and reared and fallen over several times while being ridden. Nobody has been hurt – yet – but I know that this behavior is very dangerous to a rider, and Susannah says she is not sure I will ever again be safe to ride. The thing is, I am not sure, either, as the blow-ups are as sudden and scary for me as they are for the humans around me. If I could control myself, I would. While I was depressed when I arrived, I am becoming stronger and healthier. In spite of this physical improvement, I more easily lose control. I guess Susannah is right. I have become an angry mare. I have been used, disrupted, my voice has been taken, the only purpose I've ever known – racing – is gone, and even though I have come to hate that seductive, addictive sport, I am angry at how things have turned out. So I act out, and then I feel guilty for behaving that way. I feel confused, and angry, and sad, and what is worse, I am not really certain what I *do* want. The thing is, I have never really had any choice in what I do, so how could I know now?

The horses here tell me that what they want is to find a human who loves them and will adopt them. This seems foreign to me. Love? Adoption? Humans don't love, they use, they expect something from horses, they don't just let a horse *be*. But one horse told me that when you find the right human, there is love and respect and you find that you actually want to do what the human wants, and just be with that human because they speak to your heart. He said it is a magical thing when you choose the human and the human chooses you back, and when it happens, you will just *know*.

I am not sure I believe in magic such as this, but I do know that my friend was soon led away by a human I had

11

not seen before, and he seemed happy to be leaving with the girl. He chose his human. I see no choices ahead for myself.

———————

Susannah is talking to a staff member. She is talking about me. I feel frustration leak out in her voice. "I know there is a great horse in there. She has moments of sweetness, and she is very smart. But nothing we have done so far has really reached her. This mare is spent, joyless, without hope, and at this point in time she is too dangerous to ride. She needs time to discover who she really is. She needs a steady environment with someone who will love her, make no demands of her, just let her be. People come here looking for a horse to ride, to jump, for dressage, but not just to have a horse to look at. I know she could have so much to give. If only... We are running out of options."

-3-

I Make a Choice

A lovely horse is always an experience. It is an emotional experience
of the kind that is spoiled by words.   *- Beryl Markham*

I have been at Secretariat Center several months now. I am physically better, stronger, but still anxious and unsettled. Horses come and go, the general environment at the Horse Park can sometimes be noisy, and I can't help but remember racing with dread. Susannah said she is running out of options. What does that mean? Are they going to send me back to the track? I cannot bear the thought. I resolve to try harder than ever to be very good. I would like to find a human for myself.

September 3, 2016. Today Susannah seems excited about something. She says someone is coming to meet me, and spends a little extra time with the grooming, in spite of my pawing and grinding my teeth (I know I pledged to be extra good, but it is so *hard*). I see Susannah approaching with two other humans, a man and a woman. The man is tall, bearded, smiling, and his eyes are kind. But it is the woman who commands my attention. She is slender, petite, smiling and laughing, but it is her eyes... I have never been looked at like that. I have seen eyes look at me with happiness, admiration, kindness, calculation, or indifference, but for the first time I see a human look at me with eyes full of pure love and joy. Something inside me unclenches and I sigh, and as she puts her head next to mine, I press my forehead to her chest, just listening to her heart. I hear Susannah gasp, saying "I have never seen her do that! I think this angry mare has opened her heart." I realize that the woman is stroking my neck, face, and ears, and I actually don't mind. Is this the magic? Is this real?

I learn that the woman is Tiffany, and the man is her husband, Elliott. They have traveled from Indiana to see me, and Tiffany is asking Susannah if she can ride me. Susannah tells Tiffany she could ride for a short time, but cautions her that I am unpredictable, and would need to stop if I gave the slightest sign of tension. I realize I have chosen her, and I want her to choose me in return, so I behave better than I have since coming off the track. It is a good ride and Tiffany is happy and laughing, and I am certain she has chosen me, too. I look forward to going with her.

But as Tiffany and Susannah talk, I sense some sadness in her voice, a chill of doubt. Tiffany is telling Susannah that she already has a horse and does not believe she can afford another. Also, she is not sure that there is room at her home barn for me, and would have to work it out with the barn owner.

Susannah asks her to consider fostering me, stating that it might be possible to get other humans to help bear the cost. She points out that I need to have an extended time when I am not ridden, but just loved and pampered and allowed to rest, and that Tiffany is the only person she has seen who has really connected with me. It is true that Tiffany is the only one I have connected with, but I do not understand the rest. The only thing I come to realize is that Tiffany and Elliott are leaving. Without me. Wait, don't go! I chose you! I know you chose me! I could feel it. It *was* magic. You were joyous when you met me. I could tell you were sad to leave me behind. If you could not take me with you, if you already have a horse, why did you even come here? I don't understand. Did I do something wrong? Please come back!

But she is gone. And I stay on at Secretariat Center. Susannah and the others are kind to me, but I don't feel their hearts like I felt Tiffany's. I don't want to feel again.

Starlight chooses Tiffany

Some weeks have passed since Tiffany came. It is now November 18, cold and stormy, and something is going on. Susannah puts my halter on and walks me toward a woman I have never met. We are walking toward a trailer. A trailer! The last time I was in a trailer, it brought me here from the world of the track. Susannah gave up on me! She is going to send me back to the track, I just know it! No! I won't go! I break away from them and run, my lead rope dragging behind me. I feel panicked, I don't know where to go, there are fences everywhere, and I'm so confused. They manage to catch me and they lead me to the trailer again. Susannah is saying something about Tiffany, but it makes no sense. She left me. She is not here. I fight and pull, they give me something that makes me feel weak, but I still resist. After over two hours of panic and battle, I find myself in the trailer. I give up.

We travel for several hours. It is dark, late at night, when the trailer backs up to an arena. I hear and smell horses, but it smells and sounds different than a track barn or training barn. Where have they brought me? And then I hear Tiffany's voice! Am I dreaming? I want to whinny, but can call only in a soft nicker, and I hear her answer. And then I smell her and feel her touch – she's real! She is in the trailer with me! The trailer did not take me back to the track, it brought me to Tiffany! She did not abandon me. The magic *is* real. I chose her, she chose me, and I can feel her heart.

Dawn M. Smith

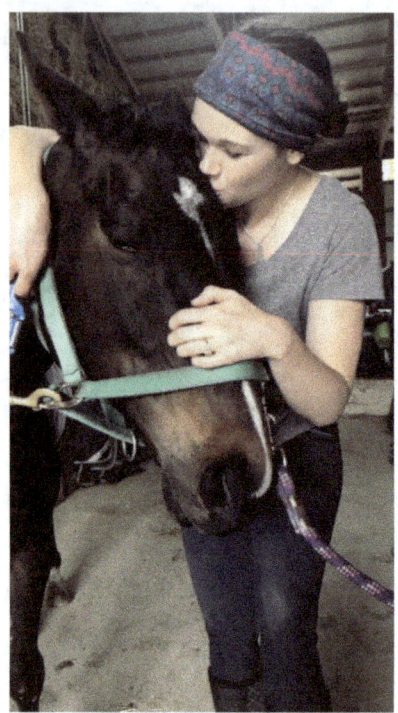

Starlight with Tiffany, home in Indiana

-4-

Home in Indiana

A horse doesn't care how much you know until he knows how much you care - Pat Parelli

Some people talk to animals. Not many listen, though. That's the problem. - A.A. Milne, Winnie the Pooh

Tiffany guides me off the trailer, into the arena at a boarding farm in central Indiana. I see Elliott, and several other humans I have not yet met. I discover the woman who brought the trailer is Carol, the owner of this farm. Tiffany is laughing and crying at the same time and I feel her heart overflowing with the joy that shows in her eyes. If I were not so exhausted from struggle and panic and travel I would be showing some joy, too, but all I can do at the moment is stand and look around. I find that I am in an indoor riding arena, attached to a barn that I can just see through a gate. I cannot see other horses directly, but I can hear them and smell them, so I know I am not alone. The arena has large sliding doors on each side, but they are closed due to the cold, stormy weather. They move the trailer out, so the large door can be closed, blocking the wind and cold rain. I am relieved to see the trailer leave and the door close; I can now believe that I am staying here, at least for a while, and it is not a track. Tiffany is here, so I am happy.

Tiffany says the other humans here are her parents, Bob and Liza, and Elliott's mother, Dawn. They all seem so happy to see me. I just feel tired and bewildered. I hear Tiffany and Carol talking. Apparently, the original plan was for me to be taken to an outdoor paddock with some other mares. But it is now later than planned, dark and cold and storming, and it would not be possible to see if I am safe with the other mares in the paddock overnight. All the stalls in the barn are full. Tiffany asks if it is possible for me to stay in the arena tonight. Carol is not comfortable with that, as it could be hazardous to me to just let me wander all night. Dawn asks if they could use the jump stanchions and rails to construct a temporary stall in a corner of the arena, and said she and Tiffany could return very early in the morning to clean everything up and take me to the paddock. Carol agrees to this plan.

Tiffany, Elliott, Dawn, Bob, and Liza all start moving things to construct a temporary stall. While they do that, I start exploring the arena. I see a huge ball in one corner. It looks like a giant beach ball. I push it, it rolls. I push it some more, then I turn around and back into it and kick it gently, trying to figure it out. I hear laughter and realize all the humans think this is terribly funny. What? I'm a racehorse. This giant ball is something new, different, without being threatening. It smells harmless, I can tell other horses have been in contact with it, so I want to know more about it. Tiffany comments that she is so pleased that I don't seem afraid. Honestly, after the panic of thinking I was going back to the track, and the relief of being wrong, I have no fear left for anything here tonight. I am just tired. And as I see you just about have my stall constructed, I will just come on over and bed down.

As I enter the opening into the stall, without any prompting, they all break out in laughter again. "Look at that, she doesn't have to be led in", says Dawn. "She just knows all this is for her." Elliott places the last bar behind me, to close me in. "She's so smart!" says Tiffany. Smart? This is clearly a stall you've built, I am the only horse in the arena, so of course it is for me. May I go to sleep now?

A little hay and a bucket of water are placed nearby, and the lights go out.

As good as their word, before sunrise, Tiffany and Dawn return. The storm is over, it is still cold, but is relatively warm and protected here in the arena. Tiffany turns me back into the larger arena while the two of them deconstruct the temporary stall and clean up all evidence of me having been there. Tiffany leads me to the crossties in the barn and starts grooming me. I have rested, so am no longer exhausted. Although I am delighted to be with Tiffany, I feel the old anxiety and tensions returning. Dawn is trying to touch my face. I can barely tolerate Tiffany doing that. I don't know if I can trust Dawn. I start pawing. Dawn seems to understand, talks soothingly, and stops trying to touch my face. She has brought carrots, but I reject them. Tiffany offers me cookies and horse treats, but I reject those, too. It is all just a bit overwhelming. New place, new horses, new humans – I need some time to adjust. I have been shuffled to so many places that I cannot completely trust that this will last. I think I trust Tiffany – we chose each other – but can I trust that it will last? I grind my teeth and paw the ground with anxiety.

Once it becomes light outside, Tiffany and Dawn walk me outside and I get my first good look at my new home. The land is flat in all directions, different from the hills at Secretariat Center. I see the arena and the barn at the side of a gravel drive, and the drive continues past the barn far into a field. On the side away from the barn is a strip of grass edged by a line of trees and shrubs. I can see a large farm field beyond the trees. As we walk down the gravel drive, I see a circular pen to the left, and several paddocks beyond that, with several horses or ponies in each. As we pass the field by the circular pen, there is a paddock with a number of ponies in it, and then another paddock with some mares. Beyond all the paddocks is a large farm field, and the line of trees turns to edge that field, with a train track beyond that. Overnight, I learned that trains run frequently there, huge, long, thundering freight trains that generally move very fast. But, the noise doesn't really bother me – at least it is not the noise of the racetrack.

Tiffany and Dawn lead me into the paddock with the mares, and Tiffany says they are Abbey, Jill, Callie, and Eleanor, four of the school horses here. Tiffany removes my halter and turns me loose. The mares, especially Abbey, make it clear to me that this is their paddock, and I am not part of the herd. They buck and prance around, but don't really try to bite or kick. It is just that Abbey moves the other mares away from me, and they block my access to the roll of hay. Tiffany is concerned, and makes sure that the roll is split into more than one area, so I can have access to eat, too. But I feel the old depression return, and I prefer to be apart from the others. I am glad to be with Tiffany, but I am afraid this will all go away; a temporary stop like every other place in my life. I stand in a corner of the paddock and just watch.

Tiffany has been coming to see me every day, Dawn less frequently, but I am beginning to feel a routine. The mares have finally accepted me, though I still prefer to stand separate from them. Tiffany talks to me, grooms me gently, encourages me to accept her touch, and I am beginning to find that I don't resist her touch, even to my ears and face. I still don't trust the touch of others, but Tiffany's touch is warm and welcome. They continue to offer me carrots and other treats, and I have even sampled them a few times recently. I find they are surprisingly good! Tiffany does not try to ride me. In fact, the only thing she seems to want from me is to spend time with me and talk to me. She seems to listen to me, too, because when I cannot control my anxiety and I start to paw the ground or shake my head, she does not scold me, but stops what she is doing, gives me a pat, speaks to me calmly, and gives me time to calm myself. Nobody else has ever listened to me quite like this.

-5-

Lola

Somewhere in time's own space
There must be some sweet pastured place
Where creeks sing on and tall trees grow
Some paradise where horses go
For by the life that guides my pen
I know great horses live again
- *Stanley Harrison*

A horse is an angel without wings - *unknown*

December 11, 2016. I have been here about three weeks now. Today is overcast, damp, cold, but little wind. Since there is some drizzle off and on, I expect Tiffany to take me inside the arena to work, but she seems very subdued today as she takes me out of the paddock, turns away from the barn and leads me far down the tree line to an open patch under the trees. There is a stone there with some writing on it. Tiffany stops, begins to cry softly, and tells me of Lola.

Tiffany had wanted a horse of her own, for as long as she could remember. In her teen years, she had started taking riding lessons at a stable close to her home. Over that time, she developed a close friendship with the owner of the stable, who allowed her to come and ride some of the horses to keep them exercised. There was one in particular, a thoroughbred mare, like me, rehomed from the track, like me, named Lola's Lady. Tiffany described her as tall, rich bay in color, with a crooked star on her forehead that is very similar to mine. Tiffany fell in love with Lola, and it was her dearest wish to someday own her.

One year ago today, Tiffany and Elliott bought Lola, and soon after that, brought Lola here. Tiffany came every day and her happiness grew as she rode Lola, hardly believing her good fortune to have Lola as her own. Tiffany rode her in the arena, outside through the fields, exploring the area together, and felt she was flying as they would canter or gallop. She looked forward to many years of happy times with Lola.

Last summer, an extreme thunderstorm swept through about 4 a.m., sudden, unpredicted, with high winds and heavy lightning. Tiffany, awakened by the thunder, knew Lola was in the paddock overnight. She was concerned that Lola would be frightened by the storm. She and Elliott came out in the storm to bring Lola inside. To their horror, they found Lola on her side in the paddock, dead, struck by lightning. The anticipation of many happy years was abruptly reduced to only eight months. The shock of Lola's death left Tiffany uncomprehending and lost, and now, a year after adopting Lola and just a few months since the storm, she still grieves the loss. This spot is Lola's grave. Tiffany buries her face in my neck as she cries and I do not object. Somehow, it feels like my presence is helpful to her, and I find I want to help her if I can. I listen as she tells me about her dream horse…

-6-

Dream Horse

A pony is a childhood dream. A horse is an adulthood treasure   *- Rebecca Carroll*

You are and always have been my dream   *- Nicholas Sparks*

Only in darkness can you see the stars and only in sadness would we find Starlight.   *- Tiffany*

Tiffany's voice is soft as she speaks of the past. "When Lola died, I was lost and alone. I tried to make sense of it as my friend Sammie let me hug her mare Gracie and talk through my grief. 'Sammie', I said, 'did you know that when I was a girl I dreamed that someday I would own a black Morgan mare with a white star and stripe and a left hind sock? For years I wrote about her in my journals, sketched her and signed my name with her horse head. Her name was Starlight. Maybe it's time to find my Starlight now? But she won't be a Morgan. I want another thoroughbred'." Tiffany pauses, remembering.

I am stunned when I hear my name. I thought when Tiffany said she wanted to tell me of her dream horse, that she was going to tell me more about Lola. But, the dream horse of her childhood had my name! That's impossible, isn't it?

Tiffany continues, "A friend suggested that I check out the website for Secretariat Center, since they rehome thoroughbreds. So, I checked the website, and the very first horse I saw was a nearly black 8 year old mare, with a star on her forehead, white stripe on her face, and left rear white fetlock, named Rena Starlight. You. Your picture stole my breath. My dream horse was standing right there. I emailed immediately and told them my story and why I felt you are part of my story, too. I did not hear back from Susannah right away, and before I did hear back, another friend told me of a thoroughbred mare name She's a Good Girl. As soon as I met her, I knew she was right for me, and Elliott and I adopted her. I call her Sage, because it means wise, but also means a healing plant, and she has helped me heal from the loss of Lola."

"I did not forget about you, Starlight. But I thought my childhood dream was only that – a dream. Then I heard back from Susannah, and she told me your history and the challenges you were facing. She told me that she was sure you were not the riding horse I was looking for. But she was also captivated by my dream and the remarkable similarity to you, and she said I was welcome

29

to come see you. So, Elliott and I traveled to Secretariat Center to meet you."

"The moment I saw you, I knew you were, indeed, my dream horse, now real. Riding you was such a treasure. But I also was conflicted. I already had Sage, I did not know how to afford another horse, I did not know how to make room for you here, so I had to leave you there. But I could not believe that was the end of the story. It took a little time, and a miracle or two, but I was finally able to bring you here. My dream horse." Tiffany falls silent, hugging me.

I feel like *I* am dreaming. How can it be that a human dreamt of me before I was born? And to keep that dream for so many years, must be some kind of miracle. I have never had a human talk to me like this, like she and I are closest friends. I've never dared to dream, but if I had, Tiffany would be my dream, too. She leads me back to the paddock.

Tiffany shows Starlight her childhood journal, proving Starlight has been her dream horse since age 10.

-7-

Sage

The horse is God's gift to mankind   *-Arabian proverb*

Bread may feed my body, but my horse feeds my soul
-Arabian poet

Soon after visiting Lola's grave, Tiffany tells me she wants me to get to know Sage. "Both of you are mine now. That means you are sisters", said Tiffany. "I hope you two come to love each other as much as I love you." I feel jealous. Sage is the mare who prevented me from coming with Tiffany when we first met. I am only just beginning to get along with the other mares in my paddock. I don't want to get along with Sage. I don't want to like her.

Tiffany leads me to a stall. There is a light bay mare inside, looking at me. She comes to the door, and we stiff noses in greeting. Sage tells me that Tiffany has told her about me. She is sweet and calm, and I cannot dislike her.

But, I don't want to share Tiffany yet, and I turn away. Tiffany gives me a pat and leads me away again.

———————

Over several weeks, I am introduced gradually to Sage, and I grow to like her. She tells me her history. Like me, she was raced in a number of claiming races, but she never felt the same burning desire as I did, to race to win. She raced only 9 races in 2011, winning twice, two seconds and one third. Her owner decided she did not have great promise as a race horse and she was retired from racing. Eventually, she came up for adoption through a thoroughbred rehoming center similar to Secretariat Center, and when Tiffany lost Lola, a friend of Tiffany's found Sage and arranged for them to meet. Tiffany fell in love with Sage and adopted her not long after losing Lola. Sage and I share a racing past, and now we share Tiffany. It turns out we are actually cousins, as we have a common grandsire. Now we are adoptive sisters.

Sage tells me that Tiffany rides her nearly every day, and she feels privileged to let her ride. I tell Sage of my anxiety and that sometimes I cannot control myself when I am ridden, so Tiffany has not tried to ride me since the one time at Secretariat Center. I further explain that the thought of being ridden again makes me tense up, and I don't know if I can ever get over it. Sage tells me Tiffany will give me the time I need, and she hopes that someday I will conquer my fear so I can have the privilege of carrying Tiffany again. "Sage" is a good name; she does seem wise, and I can understand why Tiffany says she helps her to heal. I think her calmness and sweetness are helping me to heal, too.

Tiffany takes us out to graze together frequently now, and I enjoy being with Sage. We sometimes nearly knock heads trying to get to the same patch of clover. Sometimes, Tiffany turns us loose in the arena together, and we chase each other with abandon. I can rear and run and just feel free with Sage, and it is loosening something inside that has been so tight I did not even know it was there, but has certainly been causing much of my anxiety. With Sage, I am learning to play, which I don't remember doing since I was just a foal. When it rains out, puddles are left, and Sage and I love to splash in the water and roll in the mud, much to Tiffany's annoyance, but she laughs as she scolds us.

Sage stays in a stall in the barn most of the time, just getting turned out into a paddock occasionally. Otherwise, she is out of the stall only when Tiffany comes to ride her. I am outside all of the time, except when Tiffany brings me in briefly to groom or train me. I love being outside. Sage tells me she would like to be outside more. I think Tiffany is realizing that Sage would like to be outside more, as she watches us play together. She says she is considering letting Sage join me in the paddock all the time. We both are excited at that prospect. I may have been reluctant to meet Sage at first, but now I know something I have never known before. I have family, and having family is a precious, healing gift.

Sage and Tiffany

-8-

Bandit

In the steady gaze of the horse shines a silent eloquence that speaks of love and loyalty, strength and courage. It is the window that reveals to us how willing is his spirit, how generous his heart. - Author unknown

Recently, Tiffany and Sammie were talking about how excited they were to hear how well Bandit was doing. I had not met anyone named Bandit, so I asked Sage. She told me that I had never met Bandit, but he is one of the reasons I am able to be here now; so I learned Bandit's story.

There are quite a few school horses at this farm, used in riding lessons. Bandit was one of them, a gray thoroughbred gelding, a calm and reliable school horse, and he loved children. But he had developed a problem with his knees, and Carol felt he could not continue as a school horse, being ridden frequently by many people. This was occurring at the same time that Tiffany and

Elliott were trying to find a way to foster me, and one of the problems was that there was no room here for another horse. Carol asked Susannah at Secretariat Center if there might be any chance that they could accept Bandit, to find a home for him, and that would open a spot for me.

When Susannah heard that Bandit was gray, she said she had been contacted recently by a family in Greenwood, Indiana, which is less than an hour away from here. They were looking for a gentle horse for their special-needs son, and specifically wanted a gray thoroughbred. None of the horses then at Secretariat Center fit what they were looking for, but Susannah asked if she could tell the family the information about Bandit, so they could come see him here. Carol said that would be great.

The family came to meet Bandit, and Tiffany was present as well, since she was hopeful this might work out to find Bandit a new home and to open a spot for me. Tiffany is a pediatric nurse, and to her surprise, she knew the little boy and the family, because she had once been the nurse for the little boy. The family was pleasantly surprised and said something about fate. The little boy met Bandit, and it was clear to all who were watching that the boy and Bandit chose each other.

The boy's parents were very interested in adopting Bandit, except that they were worried that Bandit's knee problems would worsen. When Susannah heard this, she called a veterinarian she knows, related the story and how it would help two horses and a special needs child if the knee problem could be resolved. The vet said that if Bandit could be brought to Secretariat Center, he would fix Bandit's knees, and six weeks after surgery, they could come get him and the boy could have Bandit as his own.

Susannah told the family, and they were thrilled. Tiffany was thrilled as well, since this meant a spot would open up for me to come here. She was so excited when she told Sage about it. Susannah and Carol worked out all the details, and in November, Carol loaded Bandit into the trailer and took him to Secretariat Center, and brought me here on the return trip. Tiffany and Sammie are so excited today because the surgery for Bandit was successful and he is back with his new family. Tiffany recently spoke with the family, and Bandit and his boy are doing great.

Upon learning Bandit's story, I try to absorb it all. I suddenly realize that this explains why Tiffany could not take me with her from Secretariat Center right away, and I am amazed at the series of events that had to occur to open the way for me to be brought here. The boy's family had mentioned fate. Tiffany had said it took some time and a couple miracles to get me here. I am beginning to believe in magic and miracles. Maybe another miracle will happen to help me overcome my fears.

-9-

Dance Lessons

When your horse follows you without being asked, when he rubs his head on yours, and when you look at him and feel a tingle down your spine… you know you are loved - John Lyons

The horse moved as a dancer which is not surprising. A horse is a beautiful animal, but he is perhaps most remarkable because he moves as if he always hears music - Mark Helprin, A Winters Tale

Tiffany has not ridden me since I have been here, but she has been working with me in other ways. She has been grooming me and helping me learn to be calmer and more accepting of touch. She gives me treats when I am good, and I now know that treats are highly desirable. Initially, she took me to the arena and just turned me loose, letting me explore and run if I wanted to. Then, she started working me on the lunge line, a long lead that allows me room to circle around her at all paces, but is still connected to my halter. The lunge line confused me at first, especially going clockwise. Racetracks in America always turn counterclockwise, and it felt very unnatural to turn clockwise. Walk and trot were not too bad, but at the canter, I got my feet all mixed up. I would try to take my left lead, as that was what I was used to, but that is quite uncomfortable going clockwise, so I would try to switch leads. But I would get mixed up and be on right lead in front and left in back and that did not work *at all*, and then I would just start hopping and kicking. Have you ever actually thought about how you walk and then suddenly not been able to walk naturally at all? Yeah, it was like that, except with four feet.

Tiffany has been patient with me, and it has started getting easier, although I still prefer counterclockwise. Tiffany has added target training with a clicker. She showed me a funny stuffed animal on a stick. I was curious. When I reached to touch it with my nose, I heard a click, and she praised me and gave me a treat. It didn't take me long to figure out that if I see the animal (the target) and touch it with my nose, I hear a click and get a treat. By now, I am completely enamored of treats. I rejected them in the past – what was I thinking? Treats are very tasty! We are now to the point that Tiffany can put the target across the arena, and I will go to it and claim my treat. This is something that is different from anything I have done before, and Tiffany seems to enjoy the game. I enjoy the treats.

Today, Dawn suggested that I might like to learn to dance. She said something about seeing videos of horses and humans line dancing. It makes little sense to me, but she brings carrots, which I now crave. Dawn starts by leading me into the arena, standing by my head and telling me to "stand". I can smell those carrots and I prance about a bit, but when I finally stand still, she praises me and gives me a carrot. I like this. Let's do more! She leads me in a small circle, again stops and tells me to "stand". I comply pretty quickly this time, and I score another carrot. Sweet! Before long, she says "Back" and pulls back just a bit on my halter as she steps backward. I try to circle to face her. No carrot. Dawn repeats the process, and when I take one step backward, she praises me and a carrot appears. Okay, I've got this now. By the end of the first dancing lesson, I have done patterns of four steps forward, stand, four steps backward, stand, and the carrot pocket is empty.

———————

It has been several weeks. Tiffany has continued target training, Dawn has continued the dance lessons, and I can now step forward, back, turn both directions on the fore, and stand pretty much on command. I really enjoy the game, and especially the carrots. Today, Tiffany has brought me into the arena. She tells me to stand, which I do, she unclips my lead, and she starts moving forward,

41

backward, and in circles, and I follow her closely, my head by her shoulder. She uses the clicker each time we complete a series of steps in one direction or another, but gives me treats only at the end. I hear her laughing and telling me how smart and good I am, and it is only then that I fully realize that she did not actually prompt me directly to do any of these things. She had unclipped the lead, and I was free not to follow. At any point, I could have stopped or run across the arena. But I wanted to follow Tiffany, and I don't think it was just for the treats. It is clear that when I follow her like this, it makes her happy, and now I know that she makes me happy, too.

This is new to me, being able to choose to follow, and being happy. I feel calmer, more relaxed. I anticipate visits from Tiffany, and nicker at her when she approaches the paddock. Maybe I can trust that this will last. I am surprised to find that I don't have to be afraid of new things, and that dancing is a path to happiness.

-10-

Friends

If you have gained the trust of a horse, you have won a friend for life
- unknown

I have been meeting many horses, humans, and other animals, and it is different than I have ever known before. In the racing world, I have met many horses, but had very little opportunity to really become acquainted with any of them for very long. Either I was claimed and went to a new place, or others in the stable were claimed or sold, so stability was scarce. I did get to know jockeys and trainers and stable hands, but it was generally all business, and there were frequent changes there, too. In addition to the frequent changes, most of the other horses that I met were my competitors, and it is difficult to become friends with someone who is as determined to win as you are, and the only way either of you can get the high of the win is to beat the other. Although I met many horses and humans, without stability, I had no friends, and the only thing I could rely on was constant change.

I have been here several months now, and for the first time in my life, I feel some stability and calm routine, and I think I am learning about friends, and what friendship means. Of course, the first friend is Tiffany. She is more than a friend. Our hearts speak to each other. She *gets* me, many times even when I don't get myself. I am beginning to feel I can trust her, and that is not easy for me. As I learn to trust her, I want to please her, in return for her love and care. This friendship is helping me to heal and be happy.

There are so many friends here. Elliott is Tiffany's husband and best friend, and because she loves him, I trust him, too. He is kind and gentle and always gives me pats and treats. He introduced me to their dog, Remi. She is a different type of friend. I was afraid of her at first. She is a Great Dane, and as tall as Theodore, one of the ponies here. I had never seen such an enormous dog. Elliott could tell I was nervous, and introduced us slowly over time. I now know that Remi would never hurt me, so she is a friend, too.

Sage is my cousin and friend. We are now in the same herd, and she helps me learn to be calm, as well as to play. We scratch each other's withers, splash and roll in the mud together, chase each other around the paddock, and compete for the best patches of clover when grazing. Sage is a very special friend, because she has taught me to play.

Dawn is Elliott's mother. She says that since I am Elliott and Tiffany's "baby", I am her "grand-horse". She was the first one to begin to teach me to dance, and she always has pockets full of carrots or other treats. I like having a "grandma". Actually, Tiffany's parents are also my "grandparents". I don't see Bob or Liza as often as some of the others, but it is clear they are full of love, so I love them, too. Grandparents are very special friends.

There are so many friends here, both human and animal. Sammie is a girl who is good friends with Tiffany, and she owns Gracie, a beautiful black Percheron-Thoroughbred cross who is sometimes in the same paddock with me and Sage. I love Gracie, as well as Sammie, who often comes to see me when Tiffany is working. There is the stable hand, cleaning stalls and doing other barn work, and he always gives me a handful or two of hay. Tiffany has friends here, some of whom own horses and some who take riding lessons. I share the paddock with the school mares, and after some initial difficult weeks, we have all learned to get along as a cohesive herd. I don't get to meet the school geldings often, as they live in a paddock far from mine, but we greet each other in passing when we are in the arena together. Carol owns this farm, and she is the one who worked so hard to find a way to make an opening here for me, and actually brought me here in the trailer. There is the riding instructor, the feeders, the ponies in the next paddock, the many barn horses and all their owners, as well as riding students. Some of them I have come to know well, others are more in passing, but all of it is a welcome change from my prior life. There is no competition or tension here, rather an interwoven net of friendship, kindness, and support. I realize now that Secretariat Center was also like this, and I think that Susannah and the staff there were my first friends, because they cared enough to keep me going until the right person came along. It is just that I was too tired and sick at the time to realize what friends even were. When I came here, I felt hopeless, unable to see a way to overcome my anxiety. I now know that controlling anxiety is not a solo process. It takes friends and time and support. And now I have friends.

L to R: Remi, Sage, Starlight

-11-

Finding Myself

To remember who you are, you need to forget who they told you to be - unknown

Winter is passing, the weather has some warmer days, and I feel a stirring of something different, a strength and confidence I have not felt before. Sage has joined me in the paddock, and we play together. We have now taken over as lead mares of our little herd. I cannot really say how or when this transition occurred. It has been a gradual thing, as my friends help me realize I am strong and capable. I no longer seek to be alone, and I look forward to seeing Tiffany, and responding to the things she wants me to do. Without a particular trigger to point to as being responsible for this change, there have been a couple specific incidents that come to mind as being important in this process of finding myself.

It was an unusually bright and clear day in February. It was cool and crisp and one of those days that heralds the approaching spring. Everyone, in all the paddocks, was feeling frisky, running and bucking and just generally acting crazy. The insanity was contagious, and I caught it, big time. I felt powerful and fierce and started to kick and rear. Something about rearing up triggered the memory of being ridden at Secretariat Center, falling over while being ridden, and all the anxiety of that time came flooding back, overwhelming me. But the anxiety suddenly changed to anger which completely carried me away. As I kicked and ran and reared, I felt like I was striking out at everything that had hurt me in my life, especially humans. It was like I didn't even know where I was, and when I saw someone coming toward me with my halter in hand, I pinned my ears and bared my teeth and charged. When she persisted, I turned and kicked, nearly hitting her. She yelled at me and chased me, and I charged back. The battle of wills continued until she turned and left, clearly upset. Very suddenly, the anger evaporated. I realized I was in the paddock at the Indiana farm, and the human I had been fighting, and very nearly harming, was Tiffany. I was suddenly full of regret at the way I had acted, and wanted to call to her, but could not, since I have no voice. But something was different, too. Instead of feeling anxious and fearful that Tiffany would abandon me, I felt I could trust that she would return, because I know she loves me. So, I settled into eating hay. Sure enough, Tiffany soon returned, this time wearing her riding helmet, apparently expecting another battle. She was clearly confused, but pleased, when I came straight to her and calmly went with her. I wish I had a way of explaining to her that I was temporarily insane, and when the insanity passed, something was different, purged from my system. I am beginning to believe the anxiety I sometimes feel no longer owns me. I can find a way to overcome it. Although I cannot explain this to Tiffany, I trust she will figure out the insanity has passed.

The second recent remarkable event has to do with my halter. After my crazy day, I started resisting letting Tiffany put my halter on me. I realized that the thing that had triggered the craziness was the flashback to Secretariat Center and the history before that, of racing. I wanted to put that history completely behind me, and the one remaining reminder was the leather halter that came with me from Secretariat Center. I no longer wanted that halter, and the only way I could tell Tiffany was to resist letting her put it on me and hope that she would eventually figure it out. I know my behavior was frustrating and confusing to Tiffany, but I wanted to stop thinking of myself as a racehorse, and the halter was a reminder that I wanted gone.

One day, I saw my chance. Normally, Tiffany carried halters for both Sage and myself. She would halter Sage first and then chase after me with the leather halter. I would run away from her. But this day, I saw her carrying only Sage's halter, and before Sage could get to Tiffany, I walked up and nuzzled her. I could tell she was surprised, because for many days I had been running from her. I even pushed my nose into Sage's halter to give her the strongest hint I could think of. She shrugged, fastened the halter, and I followed her happily. Tiffany must have figured it out, because I never saw her carry my old leather halter again. Instead, she brought a soft halter that she said had been Lola's halter. Lola's halter! I felt very loved! Not only did Tiffany understand me, but she was willing to use Lola's halter for me. I have not resisted being caught or haltered since then.

So, as the weather warms and the days mellow, I know I have made an important leap forward in rediscovering myself. I have passed through rage and craziness and left my racing past behind. I have a herd. I have friends, and I have learned to play. I have learned to be a horse again.

-12-

Learning to be Brave

You can never rely on a horse that is educated by fear. There will always be something he fears more than you. But when he trusts you, he will ask you what to do when he is afraid.   - Antoine de Pluvinel

We have almost forgotten how strange a thing it is that so huge and powerful and intelligent an animal as a horse should allow another, and far more feeble animal, to ride upon its back. - Peter Gray

As spring has progressed, Tiffany has continued to work with me with target training, dancing, and ground work. She grooms me, talks to me, takes me out to graze with Sage, and introduces me to humans and animals and new situations. I am learning to accept attention from others. There is a chiropractor who comes and adjusts my muscles, and she taught Tiffany how to stretch my legs. This would once have made me very tense and nervous, but I am learning that whatever Tiffany does, she means it for my good.

Tiffany recently started putting a saddle on my back when she takes me into the arena to work me on the lunge line. The first few times she did this, I became quite nervous, as it made me think of racing. I arched my back and ground my teeth, and I was afraid I would not be able to control myself if she tried to get on my back. But, she did not try, just worked me on the lunge line with the saddle in place. As I worked, I started to relax, and I realized that this saddle felt different from a racing saddle. It was heavier, and thickly padded, so I realized I was not going to be expected to race. I remembered the one time she rode me, the day we first met at Secretariat Center, the day I concentrated so hard on behaving well. I realize I had been concentrating so hard that I barely remembered the actual act of carrying Tiffany, just that it happened. Maybe it would not be so bad after all. But she does not try to ride.

Several weeks have passed and Tiffany has added a bridle, and is wearing a riding helmet, but still she does not try to ride. I still become briefly tense each time she tightens the girth – it is just an uncomfortable feeling that I don't really like. Tiffany senses my tension and is always gentle, speaking to me encouragingly. I now settle down quickly and look forward to our training sessions in the arena. Several days ago, she led me to the mounting block, and I skipped around a little. She patted me, still did not try to mount, and led me out into the arena for our workout. I started thinking about why I behaved that way, tense and edgy with things like being led to the mounting block. It was not something I intended, it was an automatic response. I realized it was similar to my response to my old halter. Being tacked up and going to the mounting block reminded me of racing, and I didn't like that feeling. I had rejected the halter, and Tiffany understood and brought a different halter for me. Tiffany clearly is wanting me to accept being ridden, but also feels my nervousness, and has never pushed me. Anxiety is an odd condition. It can be triggered by sounds, smells, actions, objects, and sometimes the onset is just a mystery. It overwhelms, it takes control, it seems insurmountable. But it occurs to me that anxiety has become a reflex, or a habit. When I chose to reject my halter, I also rejected the anxiety it triggered. I have the power to change my response to things that make me nervous. This is a powerful revelation.

I think to when Sage and I were talking about being ridden, and that Sage told me that she hoped I would overcome my anxiety, to allow Tiffany to ride me again. Sage called it a privilege to carry Tiffany, and as I reflect on all she has done, to show me love and teach me to trust, I realize that it would, indeed, be a privilege to carry her.

As Tiffany cinched the saddle today, I was only a little antsy, and as she led me to the mounting block, I tested my theory that I could choose to respond differently to things that make me nervous. To my happy surprise, I was indeed able to stay completely calm, standing square and still at the mounting block. I turned my head and looked at Tiffany, thinking "Well??" She must have heard my thought, because she did indeed climb on. I awaited her signal to move, but she just sat there for a minute or two, patting and praising me, and then dismounted. And that was it. No fuss, no nerves, but I could tell that Tiffany was happy. And I was happy to know that I could overcome my fear, even if only briefly.

――――――

Several weeks have passed since Tiffany first sat on my back. Since that time, she has ridden me several times. The first few times we just walked for a short time around the arena. More recently, we have been trotting some as well. I am learning that it is simple to say that I have the power to change my response to things that make me nervous, but it is much more difficult to consistently put it into practice. Sometimes, like with the halter, the anxiety can be conquered by getting rid of or avoiding the triggering object. But other times, the anxiety is an integral part of daily living and cannot be discarded or avoided. The choice is either to surrender to it, becoming progressively sad, isolated, and useless, or to choose to face it and refuse to let it win. The decision to fight the anxiety is ongoing, and it takes energy and courage. Some days, I struggle more than others, and sometimes I do still startle at a sudden sound or unexpected motion, and I buck or rear a little. But it is different than the blow-ups I once had. Those were desperate, rage-filled and completely outside of my control. Now, I am able to regain control quickly, and I feel hopeful that I will continue to get better at this, with time and practice. I know Tiffany is pleased with me, as she continues to praise me when I am calm, and never gets upset with me when I am tense. One thing that has developed, though, is that my feet are sore. I try to move evenly, but I cannot help but limp sometimes when we trot. Tiffany can tell, and is concerned. She was hoping that my hooves just needed trimming, but that has not helped. I hear her talking about going to see a vet.

A new day, and the nervous one now is Tiffany. I can feel her tension as she leads me out of the barn, and I see why she feels nervous. She hands me off, and I am being led to a trailer. We both remember my last time in a trailer, when I was brought here, and it was traumatic. But things are so different now. I have learned to trust Tiffany, and I am certain she is not letting me go back to the track. For one thing, the trailer itself looks different from the trailer that brought me here. It is larger and more open. Plus, I can see Sage in the trailer, calmly munching some hay, and I would really like some of that hay, too. So, I walk into the trailer with no fuss, they secure my lead, close the doors, and we are off to the vet.

I am aware that Tiffany has brought Sage along to help keep me calm and relaxed, and it certainly worked during transport. Once at the vet, they put Sage in a stall and lead me to an examination area. Surprisingly, I do not feel nervous at all, but Sage seems to lose her mind once she loses sight of me. I can hear her whinnying loudly the entire time I am with the vet, and when we are later back together in the trailer, she has actually worked herself into a lather! Who needs to learn to be brave now? I really cannot explain why I feel calm with this, when other things can make me so nervous, but the vet is gentle and kind, and Tiffany is right here with me, so I stand still as x-rays are done and the vet pronounces his diagnosis. He says the soles of my front feet are very thin, and I just need to have shoes on the front. Tiffany is very pleased to hear it is nothing worse, and we all happily head back home.

I now have my new shoes, and they do help. I am no longer lame when I trot, and I am becoming more comfortable with being ridden. I cannot say that my anxiety is completely gone, because I do still have moments when I paw or grind my teeth or pin my ears. But the key word her is "moments". Before, in my "old" life, anxiety and anger were constants, and I had only moments of calm. Now, I have learned to be brave, to face my anxiety, to trust Tiffany, and when tension arises, it no longer controls me.

-13-

Setback

If your horse says no, you either asked the wrong question, or you asked the question wrong. – Pat Parelli

It is October, daylight is shorter, the weather is becoming brisk, and I feel frisky, but also uneasy. Tiffany has disappeared. It has been over a week, and she has not been here. Dawn has come by and taken me and Sage out to graze, and has worked with me a little with the dance moves, but no Tiffany. Dawn says Elliott and Tiffany have gone on vacation. I am not really sure what that means. She says they will be back, but when? Is it just an excuse to get me ready for things to change again? I have come to trust that this life with Tiffany will last, but maybe I have just been fooling myself. I feel my confidence and happiness slipping a little.

In addition to Tiffany's absence, there is a girl named Collette, who we have only recently met. She is one of the girls who takes lessons here, but for a period of time has been unable to afford lessons. But, she loves horses, so is frequently here, even if she cannot ride. Tiffany has developed a friendship with her, and asked her to ride Sage while she is gone, and to keep an eye on me as well. I am beginning to wonder if maybe Tiffany is preparing for us to change owners. That leaves me very unsettled.

Sage has told me that she is not very happy carrying Collette. She said that it is not that Collette is a bad rider, or that she is doing anything to hurt Sage, but just that she is not Tiffany, and that leaves Sage unhappy. She said that Collette's heart just feels different than Tiffany's, and she is not sure how to deal with it. Once, when Collette came to get Sage to ride, I pinned back my ears and charged Collette, trying to keep her from getting Sage. To my surprise, Collette was not cowed by this, faced me down and barked at me to back off. I have become so used to Tiffany's unwavering gentleness that this surprised me and I did indeed back off. I am not afraid of her, but I respect her toughness. I have not acted that way again toward her, but as Tiffany's absence continues, both Sage and I are becoming more anxious and sad.

———————

It has been two weeks now, and no Tiffany. Everyone has been very nice, nobody seems to be upset that Tiffany has not been here, except for Sage, and the fact that she is brooding about Tiffany's absence has me feeling very anxious as well. I thought I had conquered the anxiety, at least for the most part. But my confidence is shaken now. I have come to trust that Tiffany will not send me somewhere else, but what if she is leaving me? I don't want to believe that is the case, but I am so used to seeing her daily that it is very unsettling to go this long without seeing her.

Am I not able to control my anxiety without Tiffany? Am I going to return to the isolated, angry condition I was in before I knew her? I have learned so much and I have learned to be happy. I don't want to believe that I will lose everything I have gained. That thought alone makes me anxious. Anxiety is circular. Once I start worrying about something, I become tenser, which makes me worry all the more, more tension, and around and around we go. I need to remind myself that Tiffany has promised to stay with me, and Dawn says she will be back soon, and just trust that this is so. Trust is still fragile. I hope Tiffany returns soon.

Tiffany came to see us today! It has been a little over two weeks, but it feels like forever. I was overjoyed to see her, and could not wait to nuzzle her and make sure she was really here. Sage, on the other hand, had a temper tantrum, turning her backside to Tiffany, and not wanting to be caught. This is the exact opposite of Sage's normal behavior. She did eventually relent, and she and Tiffany had a pretty good ride, although Sage said she felt tense and out of sorts. Tiffany then tacked me up and took me to the arena, and I felt much tenser than I anticipated I would. I was so relieved to see Tiffany again, that I figured it would all be good. But, I am also out of sorts. Tiffany mounted, and I felt edgy and nervous and jumped at nothing. This is not as out of control as I once was, but it is still something that I am not able to control today, and that makes me even more nervous. Tiffany does not push me, dismounts, and pats me and says it is okay. I don't know – is it really okay? Or have I been fooling myself that I can control my anxiety, and my natural state is one of tension and nervousness? I don't know what to think.

———————

Tiffany has been back for several weeks now. She seems to understand that my anxiety increased when she was gone. She has not ridden me as much, and has gone back to more time on the lunge line, or just letting me run and play in the arena. I have enjoyed this a great deal, as the footing in the paddock in the current weather is not secure enough for me to really run. In fact, more recently, she has turned both me and Sage loose in the arena, and we have had great fun running, rearing, chasing each other, and just playing. I have learned to play again. It was not just a passing phase. I am beginning to believe that the increase in anxiety was just a temporary phase. I really can overcome the anxiety and let Tiffany ride me. She still has not asked me to trot, we just walk some, and I still startle easily, but I find I can control myself quickly, and Tiffany seems pleased with my progress. I believe that the setback was only that, a temporary setback, and when Tiffany asks me to trot again, I will be ready. In fact, I think I am looking forward to the day she asks me to canter. Someday...

-14-

Thanksgiving and New Year

A canter is a cure for every evil — Benjamin Disraeli

The world is best viewed through the ears of a horse — unknown

To ride on a horse is to fly without wings — unknown

November 2017, this is an important time for me. This month holds my first anniversary of belonging to Tiffany. She says it is a time of Thanksgiving and looking forward to a new year, and I do feel so very thankful to be in this new life, with Tiffany and all my family and friends. I have learned to be a horse again, I have found a purpose in bringing happiness to Tiffany, and I have started to trust that my new life with Tiffany will last well into the future.

Something has been bothering Sage, though. She says she can't really explain it, but feels like she cannot tolerate the bit in her mouth any more. She still likes to carry Tiffany, but is so distracted by the bit that she backs up, turns, and just cannot seem to respond positively to Tiffany's direction when she rides. Tiffany has been worried, and had the vet check Sage, to be sure there is no abscess, bad teeth, or other jaw problem. The vet has not been able to find anything wrong, and Tiffany says she feels somewhat at a loss to figure out what the problem is.

In addition to the problem with Sage, Tiffany says that their Great Dane, Remi has developed a mast tumor and has to have surgery to have it removed. I can feel Tiffany's sadness and worry, and I try very hard to be calm and quiet when she rides me. We continue to work on walk and add trot and balance routines, and time passes quickly through the holidays and into the new year.

In January of 2018, Tiffany brings a different bridle to try on Sage. It is a bitless bridle, one recommended by a trainer at the farm. Sage immediately responds positively to it, and tells me that it just feels so much better to not have metal in her mouth. Tiffany has decided to use the bitless bridle on me, as well, and I agree with Sage that I like it just fine. Tiffany has always had a light touch on the reins, but without the bit, I rely more on her weight and balance, and I feel more relaxed. Our work on walk, trot, and balance continues.

Another change in the new year is that Tiffany has allowed Collette to ride me from time to time. She was hesitant at first, due to my history of unexpected blow-ups, but since Sage was clearly not responding well to Collette, Tiffany wanted her to try riding me. She explained to me that Collette is a friend who loves horses, does not have one of her own, and she remembers how it was before she owned Lola. She said that the kindness of Lola's previous owner, in allowing her to ride some of her horses, was so important in her teen years, as she could talk to the horses in ways she could never talk to anyone else, and in return felt free and happy. She felt that Collette could use some "positive horse time" as well.

I listened to Collette's heart, and I felt something there, completely different from Tiffany's heart, and yet so close to my own. There was a deep sadness, a quiet desperation that Collette hid from other humans, but I could feel it. I had lived that deep sadness and desperation myself. I remembered her boldness in standing up to me when I charged her, and I admired her fire and determination to overcome. So, I allow her to ride me, and we are developing a bond that is different from the bond with Tiffany, yet one that I believe to be very helpful to Collette. When she rides me, I can feel her happiness, which was rarely there at other times.

———————

It is now Spring, 2018. Tiffany has become distracted and busy. She says that the surgery for Remi had been initially successful, but that the tumor has returned, and is now growing quite aggressively. She is saddened and worried by this. In addition, she says that she and Elliott are looking for a new house with some acreage. It has been their dream (well, Tiffany's at least) to bring me and Sage to live at their own home. This sounds like something that would be wonderful, to have Tiffany nearby all the time, so I am trying harder than ever to be calm and balanced while riding, and to be ready if she asks me to canter. I am sure that if I could hold things together to canter, without blowing up, it would demonstrate to her that I really am becoming more reliable. I know it would make her very happy to achieve that goal.

It is a beautiful day in April, 2018. Everything feels right, and I know that Tiffany can feel it, too. She asks me to canter, urging me with her weight, balance, and voice. For a moment, I feel afraid of the old demons arising; afraid I might lose control, as I momentarily flash back to thoughts of breaking into a gallop when racing. Cantering is so close to a gallop... Again I hear and felt her urge, and I reach out into a canter. Suddenly, it feels like freedom and flying, and I know she can feel it, too. She does not ask me to canter for very long, but we do canter for a brief time in both directions in the arena, and she is now praising me and laughing out loud with joy. I feel I have achieved another important goal, and I can feel Tiffany's pleasure with my progress.

-15-

Beacon Hill

Nothing moves me more than when on the way to fetching my mare in the morning than the sound of her neighing to me as I open the gate —
unknown

It is now June of 2018. Tiffany still comes daily, but seems distracted. She tells me that she and Elliott have found a place that they will be able to bring us to live, but must fix the barn and fences and pastures. So, much of her time is invested in preparing the place, which she calls Beacon Hill. Her description sounds wonderful, but I resent that she cannot be with me and Sage as long as usual some days. But, she is also sad. She says that Remi is getting sicker, the tumor has returned and is now very aggressive, and she knows that Remi does not have much longer to live. Although I don't like it when Tiffany is frequently so distracted, I feel her deep sadness and try my best to be calm and gentle for her.

It is June 24, 2018, and it all seems to be falling apart. Tiffany leads me to a trailer, saying she wants to practice loading and unloading, in preparation for the move to Beacon Hill. When I see the trailer, though, I panic. It looks like the same trailer that brought me from Secretariat Center to this stable. It is a small trailer, straight-load, and dark, not like the trailer that took me to the vet to have my feet checked. That trailer was large and open and I felt it could trust it, but this one makes me flash back to Secretariat Center, the fear that I felt there, and the fear of returning to the track. Unreasonable panic takes over, and I refuse to load into the trailer. I become certain that if I get into this trailer, I will be taken back to my old life of racing, and I can't handle it. It is not logical; I know that Tiffany will not take me back to racing, but I cannot escape the fear. I fight and balk and do everything in my power to avoid loading into the trailer. By the end of three hours, I have loaded and unloaded twice, but both Tiffany and I are drenched in sweat, Tiffany is sobbing, and she tells the stable owner that if we cannot find a different solution when it comes time to go to Beacon Hill, she will lead me herself on the road, walking the 12 miles from here to Beacon Hill!

It is July 11, 2018. Remi has become very ill. Tiffany says it is clear that it is time for her to cross the rainbow bridge. She and Elliott spend the day taking Remi to all her favorite places, including here at the stable, to visit with me and Sage. I can tell she is very weak, and in pain, but her big heart is full of love for Tiffany and Elliott. At the end of the day, they take Remi to the vet for the final time and hold her close as they tell her goodbye. They take her to her final resting place, by the barn at Beacon Hill.

The next time I see Tiffany, she buries her face in my mane and cries. But she also tells me that she will soon introduce me to a new Great Dane puppy they have adopted. She says his name is Tonka, and he is not a replacement for Remi, as nothing can replace Remi. But, Remi was such a wonderful dog, that they would feel something huge is missing without another dog. On July 19, 2018, Tiffany and Elliott bring Tonka to the stable. They say he is a Great Dane, but he is so tiny. He is an eight-week-old puppy. I know that baby animals are smaller than adults, but this one looks very tiny indeed. They say he will grow as large as Remi in time, but it seems impossible. He is mottled white and gray and black, and is all ears and paws and wiggles and wet tongue. He sniffs at my nose and licks me, and I feel Tiffany's happiness, mixed with the sadness of missing Remi. I believe that Tonka and I will become great friends.

Tonka, 8 weeks old

_____

It is now August, 2018. Tiffany tells me and Sage of the progress at Beacon Hill. They had to fence two pastures, build a run-in, fix the stalls and electricity in the barn, obtain hay and grain, and find a way to transport us there. She says the goal is to move us over Labor Day weekend, as they will have a long weekend to get the job done and get us settled. She also says that we are going to bring one of the school horses, Callie, to live with us at Beacon Hill. Callie has shared our paddock since I have been here, so we get along just fine. Tiffany explains that Callie is quite old now, and no longer up to the rigors of being a school horse. She had told the owners of the stable that she was concerned about having just me and Sage at Beacon Hill, as one of us would always be alone in the pasture while the other was being ridden, and she knows from observation that neither I nor Sage like being alone. She was considering perhaps finding a pony for companionship, when the owners suggested that they adopt Callie, as she needed to be retired. That seemed a perfect solution for everyone, and I must admit that I am happy to hear that one of our herd will be coming with us. This has also resulted in a perfect solution to transfer us to Beacon Hill. As there are three of us to transfer, Tiffany wanted to find a larger trailer than the small two-horse trailer that was the scene of such a battle a few weeks ago. She spoke with the friend who has the larger 4-horse slant-load trailer that she borrowed to take us to the vet, and the friend agreed to help.

It is now Labor Day weekend, 2018. I can feel Tiffany's anxiety as she leads me toward the trailer, obviously concerned that I might balk again, but I have absolutely no reservation about this trailer. This one does not trigger any flashbacks about my racing days, and I load right in, along with Sage and Callie. Tiffany starts shaking her head and laughing, as relief spills off her in almost visible waves.

It's a short trip to Beacon Hill, and Sage, Callie, and I are eager to see our new home. As we come out of the trailer, I can see Elliott and Tiffany's house on the hill, a small barn below the house on the right, large trees running along a creek that runs through their land, and on the other side of the creek, a large fenced area divided into two pastures. The pastures are hilly and full of green grass, with a new wooden run-in at the top of the hill in the north pasture. It looks like a slice of heaven. The paddock we had been in at the stable did not have grass growing in it, and was flat and relatively small for the little herd that was there. There was really no room to run, and although we had plenty of hay to eat, there was no fresh browse. Here, it is green as far as we can see, and plenty of room to run, roll, or just graze. Tiffany has a number of friends and family here to greet us, and as we are led to the pasture, I feel something I have not felt before. It is comfort and calm and the knowledge that this is HOME. It is not a racing or training barn or boarding stable, it is home, my home, Tiffany and Elliott's home, Tonka's home. We are released into the pasture, and we all get right to the important business of eating that luscious green grass. As the day progresses, we run, kick, buck, rear, roll, and return to grazing. Tiffany is pleased that things have gone so smoothly. I am happy to be home at Beacon Hill.

L to R, Starlight, Sage, and Callie, home at Beacon Hill

-16-

Secrets

*There is no secret so close as that between a rider and his horse –
unknown*

*All I pay my psychiatrist is the cost of feed and hay, and he'll listen to me
any day. – Unknown*

Feeling down? Saddle up – unknown

Since our arrival at Beacon Hill, we have spent our time becoming accustomed to life in our new home. During the winter months, there are only rare times that the weather is pleasant enough for riding, but even if we are just in the mud lot and barn, Tiffany comes to see us daily, brushing us, mucking our stalls, talking to us, giving us our food and frequent treats, and life is now moving at a calm and gentle pace. I have caused Tiffany a couple worried moments when I managed to get out of my stall and into the main part of the barn. My stall gate was still secured, so Tiffany thinks I must have jumped the door, although there is no room for a run-up. How I did it is my secret, and I am not telling. But, it was just a couple times, and as it clearly caused Tiffany such worry, I have not done it any more.

Throughout the spring, summer and fall of 2019, Tiffany has been riding me in various places, starting in the fenced pastures, then the area around the pastures, into neighboring fields, and even on the edge of a bean field near a noisy interstate highway. I can see the waves of the soybeans in the wind, and the noise of the traffic does not bother me at all. Tiffany has been challenging me by introducing new things like walking on a tarp, which I initially did not like much, but when I found it did me no harm, I could accept it and other desensitizing exercises. I know I can trust Tiffany, and I want to please her.

Tiffany has encouraged Collette to ride me, and we have even progressed to some walking and trotting bareback. There came one significant day when Collette on me and Tiffany on Sage did some more extensive riding in the neighborhood. Collette started talking to me in low tones, opening her heart to me about deep secret things that she has to deal with. It made me cry for her and I worked to remain very calm and gentle for her as she talked and cried. Tiffany was a distance ahead and could not hear us. There came a point when she turned around and Collette quickly turned away from her. Tiffany saw the tears on my face and exclaimed, "Is Starlight CRYING?? Collette, are YOU crying??" Collette, soon dry-eyed, just said that she and I were talking out some issues, and all is better now. She clearly did not wish to divulge her secrets to Tiffany, so her secrets are my secrets. But, I could feel that she was calmer after her talk to me than she had been in a long time, and I believe that it must have helped her, to be able to talk to me and know that her secrets were still safe.

It is now December 22, 2019, an unseasonably warm and sunny day. Collette and Nicole, another of Tiffany's friends, are visiting, and all decided it is a great day for riding. Tiffany is on Sage, Nicole on Callie, and Collette is riding me. Collette feels lighter and happier than I have ever sensed before, and we all enjoy a happy and stress-free day, roaming the fields around Beacon Hill. It seems the secret to happiness may be sharing life with trusted friends. I feel a calm contentment that I never knew existed. I look forward to many more such days.

-17-

Nugget

Ponies may be smaller than horses, but their outsized attitudes make up for anything they may lack in physical size – Dawn Smith

In late February, 2020, Tiffany brought a new member to our herd. His name is Nugget. He is a pony, and although he is small, he is full of attitude. Sage and I pretty much ignore him, even though he very rudely tries to push us away from our grain in order to eat it himself. I have set him straight on that, but patient Sage sometimes lets him get a few mouthfuls. Callie, however, initially did not like Nugget at all, charging and butting him and pushing him around. He has taken it right in stride (literally!) and just kept coming back for more.

After only a couple weeks, Callie and Nugget are now very close friends. Callie, due to her age and arthritis, sometimes has some difficulty getting up from the ground after rolling. Nugget gets right beside her and pushes to help her get up. Tiffany said she wanted to have a pony at Beacon Hill, as she and Elliott are planning to become foster parents, and they want something smaller for them to ride. She tells me that they specifically want to foster young teens, to hopefully offer them some stability and positive guidance as they make that tough transition to adulthood. She also says that she is hopeful that all of us can help them feel happy and loved, as it is likely they will have some trauma in their backgrounds. One does not enter the foster system without some sort of sadness, difficulty, or trauma.

I know about difficult transitions. I think I have already been some help to Collette, as she worked through some tough things. I remember a little boy, the son of one of Tiffany's friends, who came to visit one day. His heart seemed very different from anyone else I had met. Tiffany said he had special needs, and he did not talk like other children I had seen. His heart felt pure, free of guile, but full of curiosity. I reached toward him, and he stuck his fingers into my nostrils, out of pure curiosity, and giggled. Tiffany was surprised, as I normally did not like anyone touching my face at all, but there was something about his innocent curiosity that kept me from jumping back, as I did not want to startle him or make him cry. Yes, I think I can feel these things in humans, and I look forward to helping whoever enters life here at Beacon Hill.

Nugget and Tonka (now full grown)

Starlight meets a child who is neurodivergent, on his own terms

-18-

Dragon Queen

Do you give the horse his strength or clothe his neck with a flowing mane? Do you make him leap like a locust, striking terror with his proud snorting? He paws fiercely, rejoicing in his strength, and charging into the fray. He laughs at fear, afraid of nothing; he does not shy away from the sword. The quiver rattles against his side, along with the flashing spear and lance. In frenzied excitement he eats up the ground, he cannot stand still when the trumpet sounds.
— The Holy Bible, Job 13:19-25, NIV

As winter fades and melts into the spring of 2020, all seems unsettled. Tiffany is working very hard at the hospital. She says that there is a world-wide pandemic, which is not a problem for horses, but it certainly keeps her worried, distracted, and working many extra hours. I feel a fire inside that I have not felt before. It is not fear or anxiety, but a fierceness that is very hard to describe. It has the same edginess and excitement that I felt when racing, without the anxiety. This fierceness makes me feel powerful and joyful and free, and I run and rear and buck and play in the pasture in full abandon. When Tiffany sees me, she laughs and calls me her Dragon Queen.

As powerful as I feel, I also have difficulty controlling myself when Tiffany comes to ride. It is not the same as when I was at Secretariat Center. My actions there were from anxiety and anger, and I simply did not want to be ridden. Now, I love it when Tiffany come to ride, but at the same time I feel so strong and joyful that it bursts out of me in unpredictable ways. I find it hard to stand still at the mounting block, and sometimes rear and buck when being ridden, as the joyful fire surges through me.

It was April 2, 2020, a day that was not particularly remarkable at its start. The morning was crisp and clear, and warmed comfortably as the day progressed. It was like I could feel the power of spring surging through me as I danced at the mounting block. Tiffany climbed on, and we started as normal around the outside of the pasture. Suddenly, I felt such a surge of joy that I bucked without warning, and threw Tiffany. I did not mean it, but she was off my back in a flash, and crying, saying her hand hurt and she was afraid it was broken. Collette also tried riding me, and again, full of the joy of spring, I threw her, and she bruised her ribs. The riding ended abruptly that day.

After a visit to the hospital, Tiffany confirmed that a bone in her hand was broken and shifted, and she needed to see a hand specialist. She cannot ride me, or Sage, for months, and neither does Collette come to ride. Tiffany says that Collette has moved out of state, which does not mean much to me. All I know is that Collette no longer comes to ride, and Tiffany seems sad and frustrated.

———————

In the weeks after breaking her hand, Elliott and Tiffany have built a round pen (well, it was mostly Elliott who built it, and Tiffany helped as much as she could). This is something that Tiffany has been wanting for some time now anyway, and not being able to ride for a prolonged time has prompted her to build the pen in order to do liberty training with us. This is something new. It is not like target training or dancing. It is a process of each of us learning each other's body language, and verbal cues from Tiffany, in order to start, stop, turn, walk, trot, canter and join up with Tiffany, without any tack or touching, other than the inevitable pats and kisses from Tiffany when we finish our sessions. Callie tolerates it, and Tiffany does not push her hard, as she is rather old and arthritic, but she certainly enjoys it more than being ridden. Sage and I have learned quickly, and I find that I want to respond positively to Tiffany's cues. I am, within the confines of the pen, free to choose to obey or not, but I can feel Tiffany's happiness when I respond as she wishes, and it actually becomes like playing.

As the training has advanced, it also sometimes involves going over some ground poles or very small jumps, which help to draw our attention and focus. I enjoy this, but miss carrying Tiffany on my back. I hope she is able to ride again soon.

Starlight, Dragon Queen

-19-

Redemption

Horses are incredibly forgiving. They fill in places we're not capable of filling ourselves — Uck Brannaman

My horse's feet are swift as rolling thunder. He carries me away from all my fears. And when the world threatens to fall asunder, his mane is there to wipe away my tears — Bonnie Lewis

It is now September 2020. The temperature is finally cooling after a very hot summer. Tiffany still has not ridden me, saying her hand is getting better, but she is not yet cleared to ride. I miss the rides in the pastures and fields. We continue the work in the round pen, and I do enjoy the various liberty exercises, but I feel somewhat confined by the pen. Then, suddenly, Collette reappears after months of absence.

I feel a flash of anger, pin my ears back and turn my back to her. I do not want her to touch me and I move away as she tries to approach. Tiffany tells Collette to just sit still in the round pen and talk to me, until I figure out what is going on.

Collette says she is sorry she has not been here in a long time, but that situations in her life took her far away, and she could not come back until now. Her voice is low and soothing, and as she talks, I reflect on the anger I suddenly felt at her appearance. I realize that I have been feeling guilty for the way I behaved in April, and the resulting injury to Tiffany. I have been sad that there has not been any riding for months. I had thrown Collette around the same time that I threw Tiffany, so those incidents are joined in my mind. So, with Collette's sudden reappearance and my unwillingness to own my actions in causing Tiffany's injury, my guilt turned into displaced anger toward Collette. I realize that Collette is not mad at me for my past behavior, and I have no reason to be angry with her or reject her. After about half an hour, I feel that anger dissipate, and I approach Collette and nuzzle her. Three days later, Collette is back, I stand calmly in the round pen as she mounts me bareback, and we have a short but pleasant ride in the round pen. It feels good to again feel the joining of hearts of horse and rider, and I do hope that I will enjoy that soon with Tiffany.

———————

Months have passed since Collette returned and pleasant September turned into a mild fall and then a wildly variable winter, with daily temperature fluctuations that left the ground alternately muddy or frozen. Through the winter, Tiffany kept us in the smaller mud lot connected to the barn, both for better footing and the better shelter of the barn. On those days that were sunny and warmer than most, if the footing was decent, Tiffany would take us out into the larger pastures to let us "get the wiggles out", returning us to the mud lot and barn in the evenings. Throughout this time, the footing in the round pen was the best of anywhere, and when weather allowed, Tiffany would work with us in the round pen, continuing with liberty work, and gradually returning to riding me, but always in the round pen, never outside of it.

There came a day in late February, sunny and unseasonably mild after several weeks of cold, windy weather. Tiffany was riding me in the round pen, but I was yearning to venture into the larger pastures and fields, as we had in the past. I started pawing, striking out, and tossing my head in boredom and desire to venture outside of the pen. Tiffany rather sharply told me to "Cut it out". At this uncharacteristic rebuke, I started acting worse, and immediately felt Tiffany become very tense. I tensed in response, and suddenly Tiffany jumped off my back, looked me in the eye, and said "I'm sorry Starlight. I know you're bored. But you gotta remember you broke me. You broke my hand, you broke my trust, you broke my confidence. And I'm sorry that I'm not the kinda rider that just forgets that and just gets back on, but I'm not... I wanna be, but I'm not, and while I'm working on me and you're working on you and we're working on us, we need to be patient... but you gotta remember... YOU CHOSE ME. You chose me and this is what you get.... ALL of me!" With that, she walked away from me and sat on the mounting block, with her back to me, sobbing.

I was stunned. I felt Tiffany's heart and realized that she, too, wanted to return to riding outside of the round pen, but had been so shaken by the incident that broke her hand, she was afraid and was having trouble conquering her fear. I knew fear. I had been so fearful in the past, and Tiffany had helped me overcome that fear and become strong and powerful and confident. So confident and self-assured that I had been expressing only my own desires, without feeling or considering Tiffany's internal conflict and hesitation. She had helped me in the past. I realized I could help her as she had helped me. I could help her regain her confidence if I could control my impatience and excitability while she rode me. I could be the wild Dragon Queen when I was turned loose in the pasture. I needed to be calm like Sage when carrying Tiffany or any other rider. Resolved to help Tiffany, I approached her and nuzzled the back of her neck. She got up, turned around, and hugged me hard.

———————

It has been several months since our meeting of the hearts in the round pen. Tiffany has gradually gained confidence to ride me outside of the round pen in the pastures, and we have once again enjoyed the heart-to-heart communication of horse and rider. I have worked very hard to be calm and controlled while carrying Tiffany, as she has gained confidence to venture farther from the round pen. One of our earliest rides was in the north pasture. I could feel Tiffany shift her weight to reach for her phone, when suddenly the herd came energetically bounding past. I could feel Tiffany become tense, apparently expecting that I would bolt or try to join the play, but I remembered my resolve to be calm while being ridden, and did not flinch. Tiffany immediately relaxed and laughed and praised me, and I felt the happiness in her heart.

Not long after that, she was on me bareback in the round pen, when one of the foster children and Tonka came screaming and barking out of the house, straight toward the pen, and their sudden energy was startling and electrifying. The sudden shattering of our peaceful session scared both of us, and I could not avoid a small jump and turn to face the onslaught. But I held it all in and did not move beyond that, so Tiffany was able to stay on me. I could feel her immediate tension and then happiness as she said, "Thank you, Starlight, you saved me!"

Today, for the first time, she is taking me outside of either the round pen or the pastures, along the line of maples in the wider field. It is a beautiful day, the type of day when I love to kick and rear and buck and play. But I am mindful of Tiffany on my back, and I remember Sage's calm, and my resolve to be calm while ridden. We have a wonderful ride, and I feel Tiffany's peace and happiness throughout the ride. Afterwards, she turns me out into the pasture with the others, and I start to run, buck, kick, and rear, in full Dragon Queen mode. I hear Tiffany's laughter and realize that she knows I have been calm for her. I can feel her heart, once again full of confidence, and always full of love. I know that I have been forgiven for my past misbehavior, and I feel redeemed and happy with my life. I anticipate many more such happy days.

Starlight begs for kisses after work in the round pen

-20-

Miracles

The horse through all its trials has preserved the sweetness of paradise in its blood — Johannes Jensen

In their eyes shine stars of wisdom and courage to guide men to the heavens   - Jodie Mitchell

When the Almighty put hoofs on the wind and a bridle on the lightning, He called it a horse- unknown

I reflect on all that has happened since Tiffany and I chose each other, and I now believe in miracles. It is said that truth is stranger than fiction, and I imagine that if this series of events was offered as a movie plot, it would be rejected as being too improbable. And yet, it has happened, and here I am.

Tiffany, a human who does not know I exist, has had a dream since childhood of a horse who looks like me and has my name. The horse she loves dies suddenly and tragically, and she tells her friend that she thinks she should try to find her dream horse. Meanwhile, I have come off the track to Secretariat Center, exhausted, angry, sick, and certainly nobody's idea of a dream horse. Tiffany finds information about me on the internet, but before she can meet me, finds another horse. The dream appears to be nothing more than a dream, but when she learns of my condition, and in spite of doubts, comes to meet me, resulting in a meeting of our hearts and we choose each other. This ultimately changes my life, although I did not know it at the time. Obstacles were present, and appeared insurmountable. Tiffany already had a horse, there was no room at the barn for me, and I was not very cooperative. Then through a series of remarkable events, an opening was made for me at the barn. I was brought to Indiana, to Tiffany and a new life. And since that time, with patience and love and careful attention, I have learned how to be a horse again, control my anxiety, learn to play and be happy, and even look forward to being ridden more. It has not been an easy path. There have been trials and blow-ups and changes, but through it all, Tiffany and I keep working things out. Truth certainly is stranger than fiction.

I cannot forget that my new life began in sadness. Tiffany never would have looked for her dream horse if it had not been for the tragic loss of Lola. Even the order of events is a miracle. Tiffany contacted Secretariat Center first, but a response was delayed, perhaps due to how difficult I was being. During that delay, Tiffany adopted Sage, and the response from Susanna came later. Even though initially it seemed an obstacle for Tiffany to overcome, as she was not sure she could afford two horses, we now know that Sage has been instrumental in my recovery, and has been essential for Tiffany, to have a riding horse during this time that I could not be ridden. If she had received a response immediately from Susanna, not adopted Sage, come to see me first, and adopted me because I was her dream horse, she would have expected things from me that I was not ready to give her, and I doubt the outcome would have been happy for either of us. I am struck by how something that begins in tragedy can change through a series of improbable events into something positive for multiple humans and horses. Humans speak of fate, karma, coincidences. I don't know about any of that, but Tiffany called them miracles and God's timing, and that is good enough for me. I now believe in miracles.

Even given miracles, the process of emotional healing, learning to trust, and overcoming anxiety is a difficult one, requiring persistence, courage, time, and the support of others. It requires opening one's heart and letting go of deep hurts, while being brave enough to face the possibility of being hurt again, a very scary proposition. The rewards are happiness, love, calm, and joy, all well worth the effort and risk. I am fortunate to have Tiffany's love and patience and Sage's calm support. I am blessed to have a home, with new friends and expanded herd. I have learned to open my heart to others, and have received their support to find the courage I need to face my anxieties, learn to play, and discover happiness. I have even helped Tiffany overcome fear and regain confidence, and have learned to listen to the hearts of other humans, to try to meet them where they are. I am a horse once again, and I want to please Tiffany and become her dream horse in reality.

They call me Starlight – and I feel ready to shine.

Starlight and Tiffany, a meeting of the hearts.

Dawn M. Smith

From the Author

*Of all creatures God made at the creation, there is none more excellent, or
so much to be respected, as a horse – Bedouin legend*

*The horse, with beauty unsurpassed, strength immeasurable, and grace
unlike any other, still remains humble enough to carry a man upon his
back
– Amber Senti*

I have chosen to write this from Starlight's point of view,
as it is primarily her story. This has, of course, required a
great deal of conjecture, as the truth is that horses cannot
think or communicate as humans do. But, horses do feel
and have emotions. They feel deeply, purely, passionately,
and they demonstrate a level of empathy that is almost
beyond comprehension. Horses have excellent memories,
and those memories and experiences deeply affect how
they relate to other horses and humans, as well as to how
they process things that affect them.

The talented people at Secretariat Center and other similar rescue facilities see many horses with a wide variety of past issues to overcome. Most respond quickly to kindness and consistency, and are rehomed without significant problems. Some cases, however, are more complex than others, and such was the case with Starlight. Highly intelligent, yet depressed, angry, and unpredictable, Starlight presented the staff at Secretariat Center with concern for her future. Then, at just the right time, a young woman appeared, seeking the horse of her childhood dreams, and when they met, it was a meeting of the hearts. Starlight and Tiffany truly chose each other, and through a series of completely improbable events, already underway, eventually found happiness for them both.

The events in this story are all true. Much of the dialog came from actual emails, messages, and journal entries. There have been some name changes to protect privacy of those who did not wish to be named, but otherwise, these things happened. I witnessed the minor miracle of a human and a horse who feel each other's hearts, and I saw the obvious evidence of Starlight's sadness, depression, and anxiety, as well as intelligence and empathy. As I observed these things, I started speculating on what was going on inside that beautiful horse's brain when she did things like resisting to be loaded in one trailer but not another, or refusing one halter but not another, or suddenly blowing up and then calming down, and Starlight's story started to emerge. People who have suffered trauma can be triggered by objects, events, sounds, smells, etc., resulting sometimes in panic attacks, immobilizing anxiety, or apparently irrational actions. Horses feel, horses have memories; surely horses can be triggered as well. Therefore, it seems to me that a certain type of horse trailer could cause panic, which is not evident with a different type of trailer. Or a certain halter could trigger memories that are unpleasant for the horse, while another halter is harmless. I started to consider such potential explanations as each odd behavior or challenge emerged. As I watched Tiffany work with Starlight, it was evident that she always considered that seemingly irrational behavior might have had some sort of underlying rationale within Starlight's memory. As time passed, Starlight's story became fuller, more "real", and I wanted to tell her story, not only as a pleasant story for horse lovers, but also as a way to think about trauma, emotions, challenges, and redemption. It is my hope that her story could be an encouragement for sufferers of anxiety, depression, fear, panic, past trauma, loneliness, or other difficult emotion. With love, support, patience, and kindness, Starlight has succeeded in overcoming severe challenges. She is still a fiery "dragon queen", a magnificent, intelligent and spirited thoroughbred, but she has also demonstrated an empathy that reaches out to and calms humans who have dark emotions or special needs. It is my hope that someone who reads and relates to Starlight's story might be moved to seek out treatment and support. This might include equine therapy, which has been shown to be a powerful option for people struggling with emotional challenges. I also hope that Starlight's story highlights the importance of various horse rescue programs. Whether it is thoroughbred rehoming, mustang adoption, kill pen rescue, or other types of horse rescue, these programs all need support in order to rescue and rehome these magnificent animals.

Thank you for reading Starlight's story. I hope you shine!

References and End Notes

* There are three types of horse races. The most common conception is of the big stakes races, like the races in the Triple Crown. For those, a horse owner must pay a large fee to nominate their horse for the race, and to enter into the race. The purses for the winners are very large. These are the elite races, and only a few horses race at this level. The next, and more common, level of racing is the allowance race, for horses that meet specific eligibility requirements, which may include consideration of number of wins, amount of earnings, and amount of time since the last win[1]. In both of these categories, the horse, trainer, and owner are most commonly unchanging for the long-term. In other words, there is a good degree of stability, consistency, and security for the horse, and if the horse does at some time change hands, it is not a frequent event.

The most common type of horse racing in America is the claiming race. This is a type of race that may result in the horse being "claimed" or purchased at the time of entry. The race is listed with a certain dollar amount as the claiming amount, and any horse in the race can be claimed (purchased) for that amount of money. If someone wants to claim a horse, they submit a claiming form up to about

15 minutes before the race, and at the end of the race, win or lose, the horse becomes the property of the claimer. If more than one human puts in a claim for the same horse, there is a system for determining which of them wins the claim, but the main concept here is that ownership may change at the end of each race[2]. The claiming system is an opportunity for horse owners who have "green" or unproven horses to make some money if the horse is claimed, and is also the opportunity for very astute owners or breeders to find and claim horses they feel have great promise for future racing. This may work well for the humans involved, and for some horses who are claimed early, who do well, and who find their long-term home. But for horses that are frequently in claiming races, it can result in frequent changes in ownership, and therefore changes in everything they have come to know.

1, 2. www.worldcasinodirectory.com/types-of-horse-races

3. www.thehorse.com;articles/10345/roaring

Most chapter heading quotes were obtained through internet search for "Sayings about horses"

All quotes in the story are directly from actual letters, emails, journal entries and/or conversations with or involving Tiffany Smith.

Dawn M. Smith

Acknowledgements

I have never written a book before. I have experience in technical writing (policies, procedures, research papers, courses of instruction), but writing a story for a book is a something completely different. I was intimidated at the prospect and frequently stopped working on it, as I did not think I could do such a thing. But Starlight spoke to my heart, and her story kept growing until it spilled over, needing to be told.

The process of turning the heart-thoughts into a story and then a book was supported by many along the way, and I want to acknowledge the help I received. To the many friends and family who heard me tell bits and pieces of Starlight's story over the months and years, and who kept saying "You should really write a book", thank you for planting that seed and continuing to encourage me to "just do it". This never would have happened without your belief that it was worthwhile.

I thank my sister Diane for her continuous encouragement, as well as tolerance for my obsession with this process once it really did take hold of me. Thank you for putting up with me and for reviewing and commenting positively on my efforts.

Thanks to Tiffany Smith, not only for her tireless efforts with Starlight and all the animals at Beacon Hill, but also for being a non-stop shutterbug and detailed journalist, thus providing so many pictures and specific details to show that all this is real. And of course thanks to Elliott Smith, who has supported her dream as his own.

Thanks to The Secretariat Center and all the staff there, first for believing in Starlight enough to keep going with her, as well as being willing to find ways around the various obstacles that appeared on the way to her final home with Tiffany. This thanks also goes to the farm in Indiana and the staff and friends there, who supported Tiffany during her loss of Lola, and helped her find Sage. They also worked so hard with the staff of The Secretariat Center to find a way to bring Starlight to Indiana, helping Tiffany's dream become reality. This story could not have happened without everyone involved in that effort. You are too numerous to name individually, but you will recognize yourselves in the story, and I appreciate you so much.

One of the obstacles that had to be overcome for Starlight to come to Indiana had to do with initial funding. Thank you to all who contributed to the GoFundMe account, as it was instrumental to allow Tiffany to acquire Starlight and bring her to Indiana.

Dawn M. Smith

Thanks to my friends Susan and Tori Thompson, who provided such great editorial reviews of the drafts of the book. With your help, errors were found and corrected, and the flow of the story was greatly improved.

And thanks to Starlight, who is an extraordinary horse who truly does speak to the heart of anyone who cares to listen.